WHY WE LOVE

THE SCIENCE OF AFFECTION

by Matt Lilley

Consultant:
Eric H. Chudler, PhD
Research Associate Professor
Department of Bioengineering
University of Washington
Seattle, WA

COMPASS POINT BOOKS
a capstone imprint

Compass Point Books are published by Capstone,
1710 Roe Crest Drive, North Mankato, Minnesota 56003
www.capstonepub.com

Editorial Credits
Gina Kammer, editor, Kellie M. Hultgren, editor; Brann Garvey,
designer; Tracy Cummins, media researcher; Tori Abraham,
production specialist

Photo Credits
Alamy: Black Star, 47; iStockphoto: peterotoole, 25; Newscom:
MICHAEL TERCHA/KRT, 7; Science Source: James King-
Holmes, 10-11; Shutterstock: Blamb, 12, 14, 18, Dusan Petkovic,
28, fizkes, 26-27, iodrakon, 41, LifetimeStock, 37, Mark Nazh,
33, mavo, 16, Meyta, 4, MJTH, 34, Monkey Business Images, 43,
44, 50-51, Ollyy, 54-55, (All), pathdoc, 22, Phovoir, 19, Prostock-
studio, 5, Rudmer Zwerver, 23, Salvacampillo, 53, santypan, 29,
WAYHOME studio, Cover, YAKOBCHUK VIACHESLAV, 9

Library of Congress Cataloging-in-Publication Data
    Names: Lilley, Matt, author.
    Title: Why we love : the science of affection / by Matt Lilley.
    Description: North Mankato, Minnesota : Compass
        Point Books, [2020]
    Identifiers: LCCN 2019004143 | ISBN
        9780756561789 (hardcover) | ISBN 9780756562236 (pbk.) |
        ISBN 9780756562007 (ebook pdf)
    Subjects: LCSH: Love—Juvenile literature. | Love—
        Physiological Aspects—Juvenile literature. | Emotions—
        Juvenile literature.
    Classification: LCC BF575.L8 L55 2020 | DDC 152.4/1—
        dc23 LC record available at https://lccn.loc.
        gov/2019004143

All internet sites appearing in back matter were available and
accurate when this book was sent to press.

Printed in the United States of America.
PA71

Table of Contents

CHAPTER 1

What Is Love?

SOMETIMES IT SEEMS LIKE every song on the radio, every movie in the theater, every book in the library is about that thing: L-O-V-E, *LOVE*.

Maybe certain kids in your class have been writing long, secret notes to each other. Maybe you have a friend who's suddenly gone all starry-eyed over somebody. Or maybe you've been feeling warm and fuzzy about a certain someone. At times love is just in the background, like noise in a classroom. At other times, once you really start to notice it, it can feel as if love is *everywhere*.

When we talk about love, what are we really talking about? People use the word *love* in a lot of different ways. You might say, "I love cheesy puffs!" A guy might say to his buddy, "I love you, man." Or someone else might say, "I love her, but I'm not *in love* with her." They're all using the word *love*, but they're not saying the same thing.

The ancient Greeks had a lot of different words for what we call love, including these:

- **éros** (AIR-ose): Romantic love. The mushy stuff.
- **philia** (FIL-ee-ah): The love that comes with deep friendship.
- **ludus** (LUD-us): Playful love. Think of it as flirtatious, carefree affection between two people.
- **storge** (STOR-gay): The kind of love felt between kids and their parents—love for family.
- **philautia** (FIL-aw-sha): Self-love. Loving ourselves is one of the foundations for loving others.
- **agápe** (ah-GAH-pay): Also known as selfless love. Many religions of the world believe this is the ultimate love—the kind of love that you might feel when you help strangers in need.

These kinds of love are all feelings of affection.

Some say that love is more than a feeling. In her book *All About Love: New Visions*, bell hooks writes that feelings can be hard to control, but we *can* control our actions. She writes that we should think of love as something we choose in order to nurture ourselves and others. When we love something, we want it to grow, to thrive. In this definition, love is a choice and an action that shapes our feelings.

Love. It's just one little word, but it's jam-packed with differing meanings. So are these definitions all truly part of the same thing? How are they related? To find out, let's start by looking at what's actually happening in the brain of someone in love.

DO ANIMALS FALL IN LOVE?

What emotions do animals feel? It's hard to know—we can't ask them. But we *can* carefully watch what they do. We know that some animals, including certain birds, mate for life. Does that mean that they're in love? These same birds usually nest at the same spot year after year. What if they're really being faithful to the nest site and not to each other? It's hard to say.

In her book *How Animals Grieve*, Barbara King says that in order to call animal behavior "love," you need two things: choice and grief. First, they must choose to be together. They don't need each other for food or survival—just companionship. Second, if one of them dies, the survivor must show grief. She and other writers say that grief is "the price of love." If we love something, then we will miss it terribly when it's gone.

King tells the story of Tarra the elephant and Bella the dog, who lived together at a sanctuary in Tennessee. Although there were many other elephants in the sanctuary, Tarra chose Bella for a best friend. And while most of the dogs there stayed far away from the elephants, Bella chose Tarra. They spent all their time together. Bella would even lie down and let Tarra "pet" her gently with her elephantine foot.

Sadly, after years of friendship, Bella died. No one witnessed it, but it is believed that Tarra found Bella's body and carried it home. With Bella gone, Tarra became very sad. After Bella was buried, Tarra visited the gravesite. These two creatures chose to be together, and one seemed to grieve when the other died. That's strong evidence of love.

According to the triangular theory of love, loving relationships are made up of three elements: closeness, attraction, and commitment. The different stages and kinds of love are made from different mixes of those three elements.

The city of Philadelphia gets its name from the ancient Greek words *philos* (love as friendship) and *adelphos* (brother). Love + Brother = Philadelphia, the City of Brotherly Love.

Bella and Tarra

CHAPTER 2

Love Is . . . a Chemical Imbalance?

PICTURE THIS: There's this special someone in your class. Let's call this person "C" for "Crush." You've known C for a long time. C used to seem like just another kid, but lately you've felt different. When you talk to C, you feel nervous and sweaty. But still, you *really* want to talk. After you spend a little time together, you feel all light and glowy, like everything is just fine. All your problems seem smaller. Anything is possible, as long as you can just be with this one person.

When you're around (or even thinking about) your crush, parts of your brain start working overtime. They release chemicals that make you feel all sorts of emotions. What brings all this on? To find out, we have to look inside the brain.

Inside a Lovebird's Brain

Fortunately, love researchers have done exactly that—looked inside the brain. And thankfully for them, they don't have to spend all day staring into each other's eyes and saying things like "Who's a lovey dovey? Who's my shmoopy woopy?" No, these scientists use high-tech tools to see love in action.

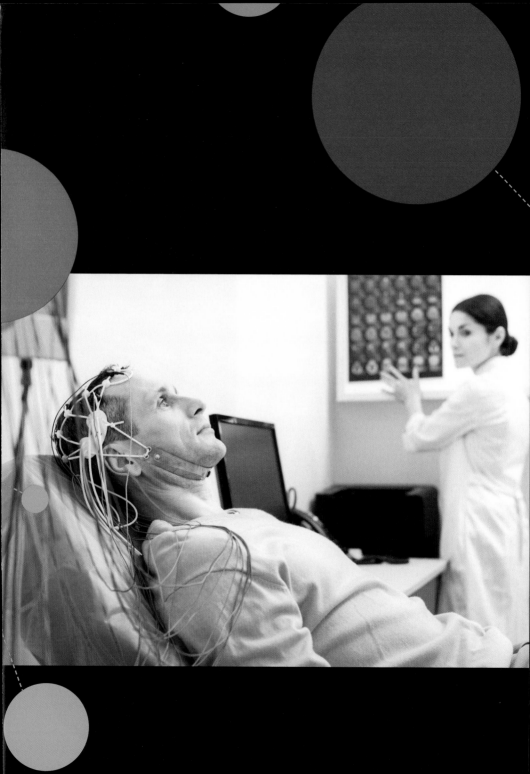

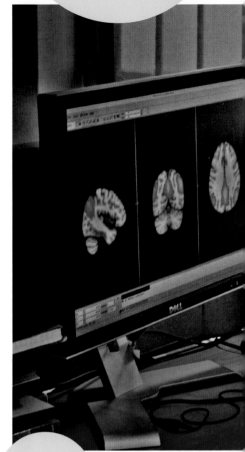

The researchers studied people in love using functional magnetic resonance imaging (fMRI) scans. An fMRI machine can view blood flowing inside the brain. Brain areas with more activity, and thus more blood flow, light up. By looking at which areas light up, and knowing what those parts of the brain do, researchers get a picture of what's happening in the brain.

The researchers asked people to think about the person they love during an fMRI scan. Which areas of the lovebirds' brains lit up? In these studies, among the areas that lit up were the parts that act as the brain's reward system. To understand what's going on there, let's first look at what the reward system is and how it works.

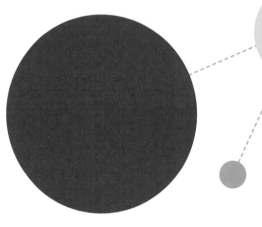

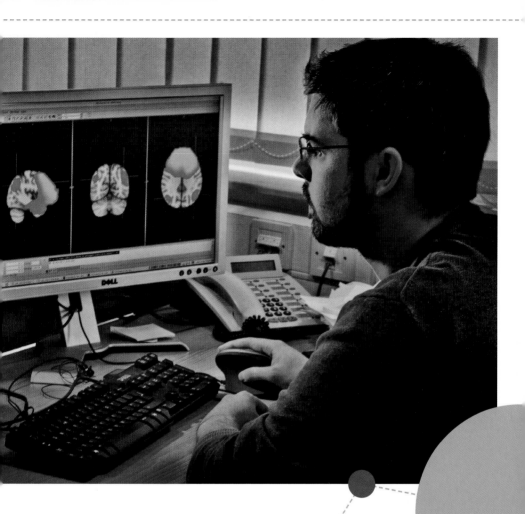

Dopamine
Flood

We experience many kinds of rewards. If you get good grades, your parents might reward you with money. Or you might get into the college of your choice someday—perhaps even with a scholarship—as a nice reward for your hard work. In its own way, the brain also rewards us when it likes what we do.

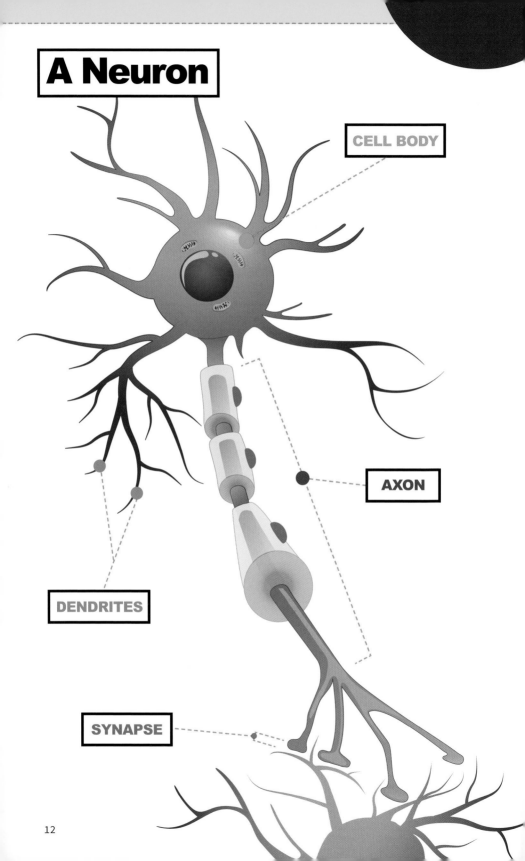

A Neuron

CELL BODY

AXON

DENDRITES

SYNAPSE

The brain's reward system works like this:

- Messages travel through neurons (nerve cells), which have short, branchy extensions called *dendrites* and tails called *axons*. Axons send out messages across connection points called synapses. The dendrites of other neurons help to catch the messages. The messages are carried by chemicals called *neurotransmitters*.
- When your brain likes something that you have done, it releases a chemical called *dopamine*. Dopamine is a neurotransmitter. Dopamine makes you feel good. One major part of the brain that releases dopamine is called the ventral tegmental area (the VTA). This area runs on instinct rather than intentional choices. As love researcher Helen Fisher says, the VTA is "way below your cognitive thinking process. It's below your emotions."
- After dopamine has been released, it sends signals around the brain. Certain parts of the brain have dopamine receptors, including the amygdala, hippocampus, nucleus accumbens, prefrontal cortex, and basal ganglia.
- These parts of the brain react to the increase in dopamine in ways that make you feel good.

In short, if your brain digs something, the VTA releases dopamine, and you feel happy. That's the reward system at its most basic. To go a little deeper, let's look at what these parts of the brain do, and what happens when they get doused with dopamine.

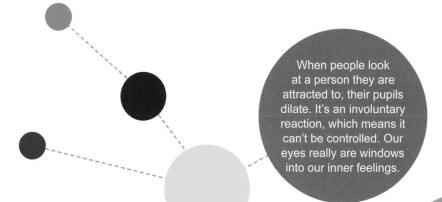

When people look at a person they are attracted to, their pupils dilate. It's an involuntary reaction, which means it can't be controlled. Our eyes really are windows into our inner feelings.

Key Areas in the Processing of Dopamine

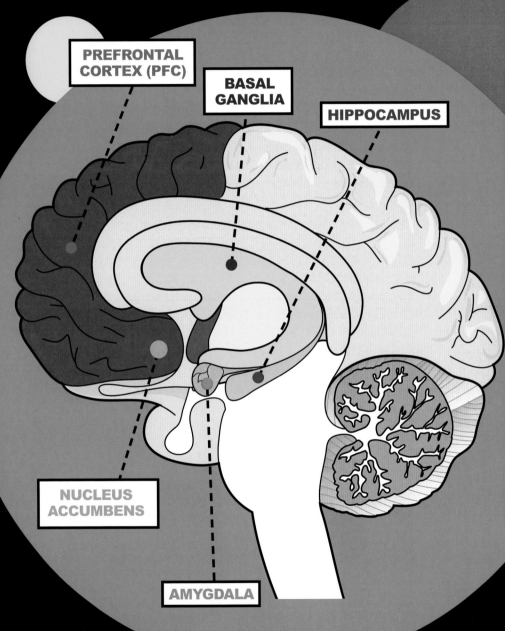

PREFRONTAL
CORTEX (PFC)

BASAL
GANGLIA

HIPPOCAMPUS

NUCLEUS
ACCUMBENS

AMYGDALA

- **AMYGDALA:** The amygdala is important for remembering things that happened to you. This includes your emotional memory, which records how you felt about something. Were you scared? Happy? Sad? The amygdala is involved with emotions such as anger, pleasure, sadness, and fear.

- **HIPPOCAMPUS:** The hippocampus helps to convert short-term memories into long-term memories.

- **NUCLEUS ACCUMBENS:** Scientists still aren't sure what the nucleus accumbens does. We know that it's a central part of the reward system, and the VTA (your brain's dopamine dispenser) is directly connected to it. It seems to be important in forming emotionally charged memories, both positive and negative. It's also involved in movement.

- **PREFRONTAL CORTEX:** This part of the brain controls your "executive functions," which include such things as planning and decision-making. When you make complex decisions, weighing pros and cons, you use your prefrontal cortex. Your prefrontal cortex also decides what is important and directs your attention. If someone offers to give you one cookie now or two cookies in an hour, your impulses might tell you to take the one cookie now. The prefrontal cortex, which can handle delayed gratification, might tell you to wait for the two cookies.

- **BASAL GANGLIA:** The basal ganglia are structures that coordinate movement. They receive information from the prefrontal cortex. They are also important for learning from rewards. In other words, these structures help you learn to repeat behaviors that get you what you want.

To review: let's say you just ate a delicious piece of chocolate cake. Here's what your reward system does:

- The VTA releases dopamine.
- The amygdala, which codes for emotion, says, "That was good." Then it creates a happy memory.
- The amygdala passes the short-term memory on to the hippocampus, which makes long-term memories. The hippocampus says, "That chocolate cake was really good. We need to remember that. I'm going to file that memory next to the time we ate mini-donuts at the fair."
- What the nucleus accumbens does is a little murky. (We don't have all the answers! We need young minds to come figure this stuff out. Seriously.) The nucleus accumbens is tied to movement, so maybe it motivates us to get up and get the thing we want. Go get more cake!
- The prefrontal cortex helps decide just how good that cake was. Should you eat some more or stop? What will happen if you keep eating cake? Is it worth it? The stronger the positive signal, the more likely your brain will say, "Go ahead! Do it!"
- Eating the cake was a positive experience. The basal ganglia prompt you to repeat the experience, so you get up and get more cake!

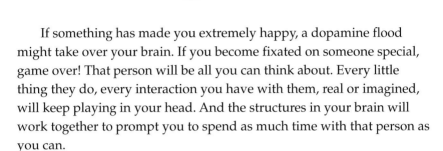

If something has made you extremely happy, a dopamine flood might take over your brain. If you become fixated on someone special, game over! That person will be all you can think about. Every little thing they do, every interaction you have with them, real or imagined, will keep playing in your head. And the structures in your brain will work together to prompt you to spend as much time with that person as you can.

You might even end up doing things you wouldn't normally do. When love strikes and the brain becomes flooded with dopamine, our judgments can be a little . . . off. You know what the object of our affection becomes? Perfect! That person is flawless. Or, if your crush has flaws, you love the flaws too. Traits you might not like in anyone else (such as nail-biting) you don't mind at all in *The One*. When your crush bites his nails, it's actually cute! Some say that love makes people delusional. Others say love lets you see someone's true, best nature.

Either way, love is powerful stuff. So powerful, in fact, that some people seem to get addicted to love. Medically speaking, no one has ever been diagnosed with "love addiction." However, in extreme cases, romantic feelings can seem a lot like an addiction. Love triggers the same reward system of the brain that some drugs, such as amphetamines, trigger. Love can lead to constant cravings, irrational behavior, powerful mood swings—it sure sounds like an addiction.

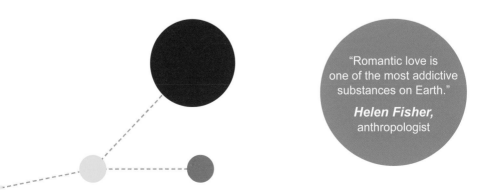

"Romantic love is one of the most addictive substances on Earth."

Helen Fisher, anthropologist

Serotonin Drop

Dopamine isn't the only chemical involved in love. Love also triggers a reduction in serotonin levels. Many mood disorders, including depression and obsessive compulsive disorder (OCD), are associated with low levels of serotonin in the brain. In fact, researchers have discovered that the brain chemistry of people newly in love looks a lot like the brain chemistry of someone with OCD. People with OCD often have uncontrollable, recurring thoughts (obsessions) and behaviors (compulsions). Does that sound at all like love? Maybe. Because of the similarities between love and OCD, scientists think low serotonin is somehow connected to the obsessive behavior that love can cause.

Pathways of Serotonin and Dopamine in the Brain

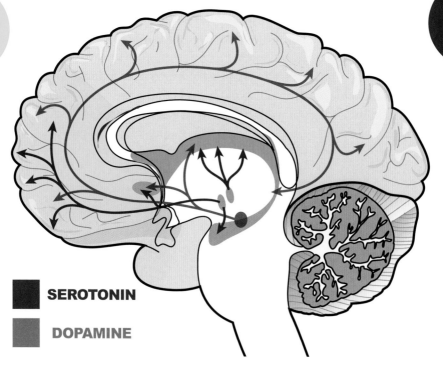

SEROTONIN

DOPAMINE

Testosterone and Estrogen Crush

Let's talk about crushes. Did you know that girls often have crushes earlier than boys? That's because girls usually start puberty before boys do. Puberty is the period when kids' bodies and brains start to change to be more like adults' bodies and brains. It's the process of becoming a grown-up (and it's a l-o-o-ng process, so be patient with yourself). During puberty our bodies increase production of estrogen and testosterone, which are sex hormones. These hormones cause all sorts of changes in our brains and bodies, from changing our voices, to making us taller, to making us really like certain people. They're a big part of why we get serious crushes and romantic feelings toward a special someone.

Evolution

In summary, love is a chemical imbalance in the brain that makes us go a little silly.

Why would our brains do that? Love is a universal feature of humanity. People of all cultures and backgrounds experience romantic love in one form or another. It must do something good, right?

Love is a universal feature of humanity.

When love works—when two people really love each other, with mutual care and respect—it creates a powerful bond. Early feelings of romantic love are like testing the water. You don't want to wade out too deep. But when two people's love for each other clicks, they might think they can accomplish anything.

One of the hardest and most important things people do might be raising their children. Some experts believe that's the evolutionary purpose behind romantic love—to form a strong bond between two adults, which helps them care for their kids. Of course, we know it doesn't always work out that way. And people can have loving relationships without wanting to have kids. But if you go way back in human history, scientists think that's what might have started it all.

Many scientists believe romantic love evolved so that couples would stick together. How did that happen? The first love most people experience is the love felt as babies for their primary caregivers—usually their parents, and especially their moms (sorry, dads). The most basic form of human love is the love between a baby and its mother (that's the Greek *storge*—love for family). Romantic love affects the brain in a way similar to storge. But researchers think it evolved later, when our ancient ancestors needed more help taking care of their kids than a mother alone could provide.

"Anthropologists have found evidence of romantic love in 170 societies. They've never found a society that did not have it."

Helen Fisher, anthropologist

Which brings us to two love chemicals that we skipped earlier, oxytocin and vasopressin. Oxytocin has been called "the love hormone" and "the cuddle chemical." It makes us feel good about other people. When a mom breastfeeds her baby, her brain releases oxytocin. Studies show that the oxytocin strengthens her bond with the baby. Hugging, cuddling, and other activities can also release oxytocin. Vasopressin is similar to oxytocin. It seems to play a role in creating long-term bonds with another person. Together, oxytocin and vasopressin are known as *attachment hormones*. They make us want to stick together with the people we love.

In the beginning of romantic love, there is less oxytocin and vasopressin and more dopamine than in other kinds of love. However, romantic love changes with time. As people in a loving relationship spend more time together, romantic love releases less dopamine. As the dopamine goes down, oxytocin and vasopressin go up. The intense passion (sparked by dopamine) is replaced by a deep, loving attachment (fueled by oxytocin and vasopressin).

So a big part of love can be traced to chemistry—testosterone, estrogen, dopamine, serotonin, oxytocin, and vasopressin, to be exact.

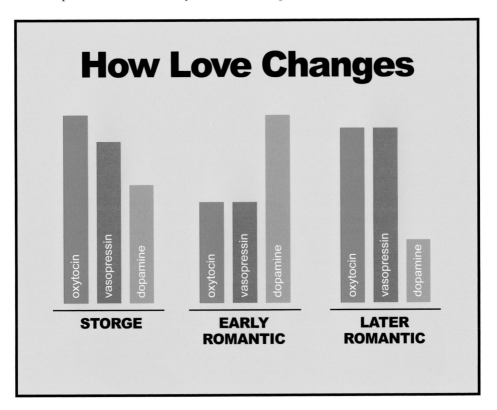

How Love Changes

STORGE — oxytocin, vasopressin, dopamine

EARLY ROMANTIC — oxytocin, vasopressin, dopamine

LATER ROMANTIC — oxytocin, vasopressin, dopamine

Diagnosis— Broken Heart

Can a person really have a broken heart? Consider this story: On July 30, 1938, Marjorie Taylor married Clifford Hartland. They were deeply in love. In fact, their love lasted through some very rough times. During World War II (1939–1945), Marjorie received a letter saying that Clifford was missing and presumed dead. Marjorie refused to believe it. Every day on her way to work, she would stop in a church and pray that Clifford was still alive. As it turned out, Marjorie was right to hope. In 1945 Clifford returned home from the war.

Fast forward to 2014. When he was 101 years old, Clifford passed away. Marjorie was devastated. She told her daughter, "I can't live without him." Within 14 hours, she died too. She was 97. It was their 76th wedding anniversary. It seemed she died of a broken heart.

While it might sound like something from a movie, broken heart syndrome is a real medical diagnosis. It can be caused by intense emotional events, such as a divorce or the death of a loved one. The Mayo Clinic describes broken heart syndrome as "disruption of your heart's normal pumping function in one area of the heart." Doctors think it's caused by stress hormones, such as adrenaline. Those with the condition often think they are having a heart attack.

So yes, a person can have a broken heart. Fortunately, the condition is not usually fatal. Most people survive and get better fairly quickly, according to the Mayo Clinic. Emotional heartache can last much longer, but time does make it better.

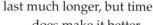

A TALE OF TWO VOLES

Prairie voles and meadow voles are a lot alike. Genetically, they are closely related. They both look like little fuzz puffs with short tails and small eyes. In fact, it's difficult to tell the differences between them. However, there is one big difference: prairie voles seem to bond for life, while meadow voles do not.

After prairie voles mate, they form strong bonds. They try to stay close together. If one of them dies, the other shows signs of grief. Meadow voles, on the other hand, show no signs of bonding with their mates.

Scientists set out to discover why one type of vole formed strong attachments while the other did not. As it turns out, the difference is found with the hormones oxytocin and vasopressin. Compared with female meadow voles, female prairie voles have more oxytocin receptors in the reward systems of their brains. Male prairie voles have more receptors for vasopressin. Combined, this seems to lead to the stronger bonds between prairie voles. Their hormones make them want to be together.

In an experiment, scientist Larry Young increased the number of vasopressin receptors in a male meadow vole's brain. The result? The meadow vole ended up acting like a prairie vole, wanting to bond with other voles. According to Young, "We transformed a meadow vole into a prairie vole, behaviorally."

By studying how these hormones affect voles, scientists hope to learn how they affect us too.

CHAPTER 3

Love Is . . . Squishy:
Romantic Love

IS THAT ALL THERE IS TO LOVE? Is it just a flood of chemicals in the brain, a bunch of neurons firing, and someone acting like a total goof? Well, of course not! While much about love may be found in our heads, that doesn't mean it isn't magical too. So let's try to feel the magic and look at what it's like when two people fall in love.

A Vat of Honey

This is the sweet stuff. The mushy stuff. The warm, gooey stuff—*romantic* love. Unlike those other kinds of love, this is the one that you can fall into, like a giant vat of honey. No wonder when people talk about love, this is what they're usually talking about.

Romantic love often starts with a crush. Someone starts to seem really, really special. Magnetic. Chosen. When two people feel this way about each other, it's game on. They want to be together *constantly*. When they're apart, they often can't stop thinking about each other.

There is a profound connection between two people newly in love. Everything between them just seems right. Loneliness, that unhappy human condition, can seem to be gone forever. Because if you've finally found the perfect person, your soul mate, how could you ever be lonely again?

And it's forever, right? Well, . . . *forever* ever? That's a long time. The cold, harsh reality is . . . probably not. The way two people might feel at this moment likely won't last forever. This doesn't mean love can't survive—it can. Just not like that.

As we saw in the last chapter, the brain doesn't keep that dopamine rush going forever. Instead, it changes. The exact path romance takes depends on the two people, but it tends to follow a pattern.

In her book *Love Cycles: The Five Essential Stages of Lasting Love*, Linda Carroll breaks down romantic love into five stages:

- The Merge
- Doubt and Denial
- Disillusionment
- Decision
- Wholehearted Loving

Carroll says couples start with the merge, when a partner seems perfect. But for some people, L-O-V-E suddenly feels like a lot of W-O-R-K. No wonder we mostly hear only about the first part, when a couple is happy and carefree.

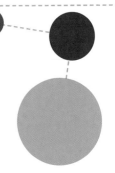

Doubt
and Denial

Let's say you've been in the merge for a while now. You love spending all your free time with your special person. But eventually, Carroll says, you'll start to miss hanging out with your friends. You may even want to have more time for yourself. Sometimes it's nice to just spend a Saturday alone, reading a good book and staying off the phone.

You might also start to notice that this person you're so crazy about isn't exactly . . . perfect. Some of your special person's quirky habits, which seemed fun at first, might begin to annoy you. *Can you please stop biting your nails?!* Some of the differences start to seem more like problems.

When someone in love first notices such issues, the lover tends to deny them or tries to ignore them. "Nothing to see here. Keep moving." Of course, nothing is likely to stay hidden forever. The doubts and differences grow in size and number until the truth is unavoidable. The perfect person you fell in love with isn't perfect after all. All those blissful feelings don't last. Whether you're ready for the next stage or not, it's here.

Disillusionment

Disillusionment is realizing that you were wrong about something (or someone). It's not what you thought it was. Not even close. It's a bummer, for sure. But it's also part of growing up. You can feel disillusioned about a lot of things in life.

Carroll points out that this stage is a bit like being a toddler. At first, babies just want to be with their parents. As they get older, they discover that they are their own persons. They want more independence. But they also want to know that their loved ones, their caregivers, are still there for them.

After the merge, where everything is "we," the "I" comes back. You want more independence. On its own, there's nothing wrong with that. It's healthy. The trick is to stake out your independence within a loving relationship. Does the relationship provide room for you to be yourself within it? This can be a balancing act, but it's the key to a healthy relationship.

For some, this stage is refreshing. You get back to spending time with family and friends and doing the activities you may have dropped when you first fell in love. For others, the return to "I" from "we" is a huge letdown. What if you don't like yourself? What if your favorite part of the merge was getting away from that "I" person? If you feel that way, then this stage can feel like a disaster.

Fortunately, there's hope. There is still a path forward for love—a healthy place for everyone to start. But for now, let's get to the next stage. After disillusionment, we have . . .

"Continue to share your heart with people even if it has been broken."

Amy Poehler, comedian, actor

Decision

Once you've seen your relationship for what it truly is, should it go on? Once the new-love glow has faded, it takes work to keep it going. For those who decide that it's worth it to stay, the next stage is wholehearted loving.

Holding hands with the one you love can relieve stress. A 2006 study found that the more two people love each other, the more holding each other's hand helps them relax in stressful situations.

Wholehearted Loving

Wholehearted loving isn't just a flood of chemicals in the brain. Wholehearted loving is clear-eyed. You know that *The One* is not perfect. But you choose to love anyway. Wholehearted loving is not based on fear of being desperately lonely. You know you can thrive without the other person, but you choose to support and nurture the person anyway. When long-term love relationships thrive, this is what they look like.

Some adults can go their whole lives without figuring this stuff out. So what does this have to do with you, who might just have a little crush? You're not trying to *get married*, right?

. . . feelings of love, both the highs and the lows, are real.

Here's the thing: Most people experience all sorts of powerful feelings during their teen years, including feelings of love. Adults often call love at this age "puppy love." That makes it sound trivial, like it's no big deal. But those feelings of love, both the highs and the lows, are real. Knowing where the feelings might lead can help you react to them appropriately. Rather than jumping into things blindly, you can see down the path and maybe avoid some wrong turns along the way.

Those middle stages of love didn't sound like much fun at all, right? But that long-lasting, wholehearted love sounds pretty good. So how does a person get *there*? Well, it all starts with the person staring back at you in the mirror.

Love can lessen pain. Studies have shown that just looking at a picture of someone you love can bring pain relief.

BEYOND A CRUSH

Sometimes a crush goes too far. It turns into an obsession. It can be hard to tell which is which. One way to avoid that is to have some healthy respect, for both yourself and the person you like.

Let's say you like a girl. A lot. But she's not that into you. If you respect her, then you have to accept her decision. It still hurts—a lot. But accepting her decision is the first step to moving on. It might take some time, but if you can get over it, you're probably still in the crush zone.

It works both ways. If someone seems totally into you but doesn't respect you and your decisions, that's a big red flag. You probably want to keep your distance. You don't have to be mean about it. Just be honest and make it clear that you're not interested in being a couple.

Lastly, if you're so crazy for this one person that your desire to get together feels more powerful than your respect for that person's decisions, then you've probably moved past a crush and into something less healthy.

Getting over someone you like is hard, but everyone has to do it sometime. Here are a few tips for moving on:

Talk it out. Find someone you trust and can share your feelings with. You might be surprised how much better you feel.

Write a letter. Write a letter about your feelings to the person you like. One of the best things about letters is that you don't have to send them! Once you get all those feelings out, you can destroy the letter and let go.

Get active. Instead of wallowing in misery, do something to distract yourself. Do something fun to take care of *you*.

Crushes are usually healthy. Obsessions are not. Behaviors such as stalking or trying to force others to do something they don't want to do aren't safe. If you think you have crossed that line, or someone else has, and you're worried about anyone's safety, be sure to tell someone you trust, such as your parents or a counselor.

CHAPTER 4

Love Is . . . Inside You:
Self-Love

L ET'S SAY YOU HAVE A CRUSH on someone. You might wonder, "What can I do to make that person like me?" The thing is, you can't *make* someone like you. It has to just happen. But there are things you can do to let your crush know how you feel and maybe inspire that person to like you too. These can be basic things, such as talking to your crush, making eye contact, and being nice. You don't have to come right out and say, "I like you." You can just talk and see if you have stuff in common. Most people will show you how they feel by how they act.

There is one important thing you can do to help your crush possibly take notice and like you too. It's the most basic thing—love yourself first. Sound boring? Maybe. But let's look deeper.

We **decide how we feel about ourselves. No one else does.**

The (Boring?) Foundation

Think of a house. What's the most boring part of a house? The foundation. It's nothing fancy—just solid rock or concrete. But without a strong foundation, sooner or later, the house will crumble. A solid foundation is essential.

Like the foundation of a house, self-love can seem kind of boring. But here's the great part—of all the things in this world we can't control, this is one thing that we can. *We* decide how we feel about ourselves. No one else does. If you want people to like you—or even love you—this is the best place to start.

But isn't self-love selfish? Not necessarily. Loving yourself and being selfish are different things. Selfish people think only about themselves. If there's a piece of cake, they want it, they don't want to share, and they don't feel bad eating all of it. As long as they get what they want, they don't care about anyone else.

Self-love, on the other hand, cares about others *and* the self. For you to take care of anyone else, you have to take care of yourself too. When you love yourself, you're in a better place to support and love others. If love is a piece of cake, it's a magical one, because the more you have, the more you have to give. At the same time, if you give it all away and don't save some for yourself, you'll run out. In order to be loved, we must love, and a good place to start is with ourselves.

How to Love Yourself

This is something we control, but it's not easy. Most people tend to be much too hard on themselves. We know our own flaws—things we're afraid of, things we're not good at, all those imperfections we see in the mirror. Sometimes we don't even want to go out because we don't want others to see all our flaws.

When we feel that way, we might forget a few things:

- Everyone else has flaws too. We just don't notice them as much as we notice our own.
- Other people are probably more worried that their flaws will be noticed than focused on picking apart ours.
- Most people are less critical of others than they are of themselves.

These things don't just sound good—they're also backed by science. A recent study found that people are bad at judging how much other people like them. In the study, people met for the first time and had one-on-one conversations. Later, they rated themselves on how well they had done in the conversations. They also rated the people they talked to on how likable and fun they were.

Know what happened? The results showed that people were more critical of themselves than they were of other people. They thought themselves to be less likable and less fun than their conversation partners actually rated them. What's more, this study was done with *grown-ups*, who've had their whole lives to get to know themselves. On average, young people are even more self-critical than adults. No matter how well you think you know yourself, you're probably still too hard on yourself. Give yourself a break. You really are more fun to be around and more likable than you think.

So if we're programmed to be so self-critical, how can we learn to love ourselves? That can be a long, challenging journey. But you can do it. Here are some ways to get started.

"Respect and love go hand in hand and work better together like peanut butter and jelly. If you respect and love yourself, you will demand that of others at every corner you turn in life."

Taura Stinson,
songwriter, musician, and author

Take Care of Your Body

Nurturing ourselves means taking care of our bodies as well as our minds. The first, most basic thing we can do is take care of our bodies by making healthful choices such as:

- Eating right
- Getting the right amount of sleep (a 12-year-old, for example, usually needs between 9 and 12 hours)
- Playing outside, running around
- Avoiding things that are harmful, such as alcohol, tobacco, and vaping

When you do these things, you feel healthier. When you feel healthier, you also feel better about yourself.

Taking care of your body also keeps your immune system strong. When you live healthfully, your body can fight off sickness better. And when your body feels better, so does your mind.

HOW MUCH SLEEP DO I NEED?

Age Group	Recommended Hours of Sleep Per Day
3–5 years	10–13 hours
6–12 years	9–12 hours
13–18 years	8–10 hours
18–60 years	7 or more
61–64 years	7–9 hours
65 years +	7–8 hours

Take Care of Your Mind

To care for yourself, you must also nurture your mind. One way to do this is to make self-affirmations. An affirmation is a statement of emotional support or encouragement. It's like cheering for your favorite football team. Self-affirmations are ways to cheer yourself on.

You might want to start your day with a "mirror mantra"—something you say to yourself in the morning, looking in the mirror. What should it be? An online search for "daily affirmations" will give you tons of examples. But there's a lot of stuff online. You can't trust all of it. Which affirmations actually work? Does anyone know? Research supports a type of affirmation called a value-affirmation.

To understand a value-affirmation, think about your values and areas of personal growth. What is most important to you? Do you value justice and fairness most? Or maybe it's being trustworthy or honest. There is no one right answer. We all have deep values, things that guide us. Reflecting on those values puts you in touch with your best self. It reminds you of who you are. If self-love is a foundation, then your values are the cornerstones—the pieces everything else is built upon.

According to studies, value-affirmations can lead to:

- **increased overall feelings of happiness**
- **increased feelings of autonomy**
  (feeling like you are in control of your life)
- **increased feelings of relatedness**
  (feeling close and connected to others)
- **increased feelings of competence**
  (feeling effective and skilled)

Multiple studies have shown that using value-affirmations can increase a person's feelings of love, compassion, and connectedness. One study using fMRI even found that when people were thinking about their own value-affirmations, the reward systems of their brains lit up—something that also happens when we think about the person we love!

Remember how taking care of your physical body can strengthen your immune system? According to research, value-affirmations can boost your mental and emotional immune system. When stressful things happen—things that might make you feel bad about yourself, such as failure or rejection—value-affirmations can help you get through it.

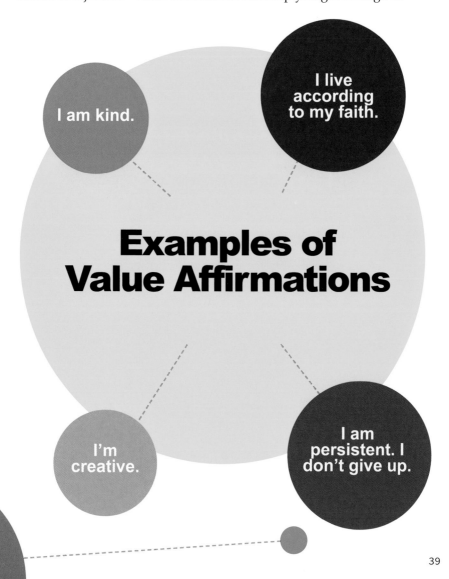

I am kind.

I live according to my faith.

Examples of Value Affirmations

I'm creative.

I am persistent. I don't give up.

DIY
Affirmations

So how do you come up with your value-affirmations? In most studies, people were given a list of values. Then they chose the ones they felt were most important and wrote about them for a few minutes. You could write about your values. Also write about a specific time when you lived by those values. To turn this into a daily affirmation, write one sentence that reflects you and one of your values. Here are some possibilities:

> **I treat people fairly.**

> **I pay attention to the feelings of others.**

> **I work hard at everything I try.**

> **I am trustworthy and honest.**

These are just examples—yours will probably be different. Whatever they are, they should be important to you. When you remember what's important to you and try to live accordingly, you feel better about yourself.

More Ways to Love Your Mind

Here are other things you can do boost your self-esteem:

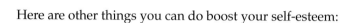

TAKE TIME FOR CREATIVITY
(using your imagination is a way to explore your world and yourself)

PRACTICE MINDFULNESS
(pay attention to your inner thoughts and feelings, and don't judge them)

KEEP READING AND LEARNING
(feed your brain)

These activities can help you to know yourself better without being judgmental.

Let's go back to Carroll's five stages of love: the merge, doubt and denial, disillusion, decision, and wholehearted loving. To get to wholehearted loving you need a strong start. Many philosophers and scientists agree that self-love is the foundation for any healthy, lasting love relationship. Without self-love, a person can still fall in love. But it would be difficult to get through the other stages of love. It would be a little like building a house without a foundation—you could do it, but would it last?

Do you need to worry about building a whole house that will last right now? Probably not anytime soon. But it's never too early to start building your own strong foundation.

DO OPPOSITES ATTRACT?

We've all heard the phrase *opposites attract*. It's the idea that people are attracted to people who are totally different from them. But is it true? Do outgoing girls prefer shy guys? Does the straight-A student want to go out with the slacker sitting in the back?

According to the research, not usually. Scientists randomly selected 1,500 pairs of people. Some of them were dating romantically. Others were just friends. They gave each pair a list of questions about their attitudes, values, and personalities. The findings? Birds of a feather flock together. People tend to stick to what's familiar to them, even in romance.

The scientists who did the study warned that if we always surround ourselves with people who are similar to us, we could end up being a little narrow-minded. Hanging out with different kinds of people can open us up to new ideas and experiences. People with different backgrounds can show us new ways of seeing the world. So sometimes it might be a good thing if opposites attract, even if it doesn't usually work that way.

CHAPTER 5

Love Is . . . Selfless:

Altruism and Compassion

WHO DO YOU LOVE? Think about it for a second. Who's the first person who pops into your head? Maybe it's your mom or your brother or sister (on a good day). It's probably a family member. Your family might drive you crazy sometimes, but you still care deeply for them.

Now think of other people you love. You probably will think of your closest friends. Just as with your family, you might not always get along with your friends, but you care for them even when they make you mad.

From the Inside Out

Starting with yourself at the center, your love extends out to your family and close friends. For this inner circle, you feel love—the will to nurture ourselves and others. What if you kept moving out from there? How far out could you extend this will? Could you feel that way toward acquaintances? What about strangers? Taking it as far out as possible, could you extend this will to your enemies? Is that possible? Or even a good idea?

Caring about others, especially beyond our friends and family, is called altruism. It's what you feel when you show selfless concern and compassion for the well-being of others.

Altruism and compassion are at the heart of many of the religions of the world. The prophet Muhammad said, "None of you has faith until you love for your neighbor what you love for yourself." The Torah and the Bible state that a person should "Love thy neighbor as thyself."

In many religions, unconditional love is seen as the ultimate goal people should strive for. According to the Bible, Jesus said, "I tell you, love your enemies and pray for those who persecute you." Buddha said that we should "radiate boundless love towards the entire world—above, below, and across—unhindered, without ill will, without enmity."

"Love is the steadfast commitment to the well-being of others."

Cornel West, philosopher, activist, and author

Many people believe that you can care about your enemies without letting them take advantage of you. They feel that if you harm someone, you are also harming yourself. In the same way, if your enemies try to harm you, they are also harming themselves. The belief is that emotions such as anger and hate actually poison the person who is feeling them. By extending your compassion, you are trying to stop the harm to both yourself and your enemies. Those who believe in unconditional love still believe in justice, but a justice that seeks to help rather than punish people. If we can help our enemy to stop doing harm, then we are all better off.

Much of this is based on the idea that hatred creates more hatred. If we fight violence with more violence, then we end up trapped in a never-ending cycle of destruction. Love, on the other hand, can break this cycle.

But IRL?

Altruistic love sounds good on paper, but in real life? Should you turn the other cheek? Love your enemy? How realistic is that? Would that just make you weak?

One strong believer in altruistic love was Dr. Martin Luther King Jr. He wrote that love is necessary for human survival. Love—including love of one's enemies—was at the core of his nonviolent approach to fighting for social justice. Before he was assassinated, King was viciously attacked countless times, with words, rocks, knives, and bombs. For seeking equality and justice, his enemies hated him. But he answered their hate with love. Shortly after his home was bombed in 1956, he emphasized that violence should not be answered with more violence, citing the words of Jesus, "All those who take up the sword shall perish by the sword." And he took it even further than that—he said that nonviolent activists must not only love those who oppose them, but also tell their opponents that they are loved.

While some might associate unconditional love with weakness, King's incredible strength through love is obvious. Very few people have that kind of resolve. King's love was not passive. He used the force of that love to fight for change.

"When we went on the freedom ride, it was love in action. The march from Selma to Montgomery was love in action. We do it not simply because it's the right thing to do, but it's love in action. That we love a country, we love a democratic society, and so we have to move our feet."

John Lewis, Congressman and civil rights leader

Selma March, 1965

Few people are ever called to extend such love to such bitter enemies. However, people like Martin Luther King Jr. and Mahatma Gandhi (the activist who led India's independence movement and whose beliefs and methods King studied) show us what's possible.

In our own day-to-day lives, what would altruism look like? Where would we even start? In his book *Strength to Love,* King described the process:

Step 1:
PRACTICE FORGIVENESS.

When you stay mad at someone, you are holding onto that anger. But if the anger is in you, who is getting hurt?

Forgiveness is hard. Like playing basketball or the piano, forgiveness is something you can practice and get better at. You don't have to start by forgiving the worst person you can think of. Start smaller. For example, maybe a classmate said something really mean to you recently. Will you hold on to your anger or try to forgive that person? Forgiving doesn't mean forgetting what the person did. Forgiving doesn't mean that what your classmate did was OK. It just means letting go of our anger and being open to getting along with that person.

Step 2:
SEPARATE THE DEED FROM THE PERSON.

Recognize that a person is more than a hurtful act. Try to see the good, the humanity, in the person you are mad at. Again, start small. For example, take that classmate who said something mean. Maybe the person was in a bad mood, tired, or having a bad day. We've all done things we regret when we're stressed, right? See whether you can let even a little of your anger and resentment go.

Step 3:
DON'T TRY TO HUMILIATE OR DEFEAT YOUR ENEMY.

Instead of wishing harm on an enemy, try to win friendship and understanding. If we show kindness to someone who is having a rough time, that person might realize what went wrong. You could be rude right back to your rude classmate and end up with a long-term enemy. Or you could try to be nice. You might even end up with a new friend.

Empathy + Action = Love?

In the book *Altruism*, the Buddhist monk Matthieu Ricard writes that feelings of altruism start with empathy. Empathy is when you feel what others are feeling. If you see someone sad, you feel sad too. When you empathize, you can understand why people act the way they do. It's hard to empathize with your enemies, but if you do, you might be able to see the good in them.

According to Ricard, empathy by itself is not enough. There's a lot of suffering in this world. If you try to relate to all of it and stop there, you'll get worn out. Scientific studies agree with Ricard. In one study, people were shown videos (news and documentaries) about people suffering. Then they were told to empathize. Under fMRI scanning, regions of their brains associated with feelings of pain lit up. They felt those people's pain. In the process, they quickly started feeling worn down.

So empathy is a start, but we also need something else. To not be exhausted by empathy, we need to feel that we can help. We need to extend our compassion. We need to take action.

The people in the study that Ricard mentioned were given compassion training. "Compassion training," he wrote, "relies on extending caring feelings—which are usually experienced toward close loved persons—to other human beings." The result? Feeling compassion actually reversed the pain effects of empathy on the brain. Instead, he said, the brains of the study's subjects lit up "in networks associated [with] affiliation and reward." The brain's reward system kicked in! The people in the study felt better. Which means selfless love isn't so selfless after all—it's actually good for you too. Kindness really can be its own reward.

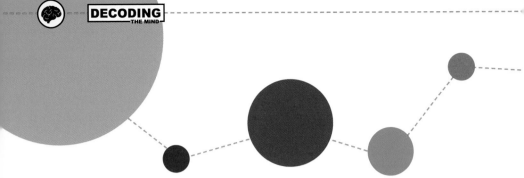

DECODING THE MIND

Extending compassion was a way for those in the study to take action to help. Here's the math: Empathy + Action = Altruism. The key here is action. In the study, the action was "extending caring feelings" for those people. The people in the study could not take action while they were being scanned. (You can't do a lot of volunteer work in an fMRI machine.) But extending caring feelings to others can take lots of forms. If your friend is sad, and you try to make him happy, that's extending compassion. If you give him a hug, that's compassion. If you listen to his problems, that's compassion.

Martin Luther King Jr. put his empathy into action through the nonviolent civil rights movement. You, too, can match your empathy to positive actions for the good of others. You don't have to start big. Any kind of volunteer work to help others can help you feel compassion.

Have you ever heard the phrase "Do what you love, and it will love you back"? Volunteering for causes you are passionate about definitely makes you happier. Small positive actions add up. Over time, this can lead to all sorts of positive changes for you *and* the world. The more love you put out, in the form of nurturing yourself and others, the more love you usually get in return.

As the Dalai Lama recently wrote on Twitter, "When you care for others, you manifest an inner strength despite any difficulties you face. Your own problems will seem less significant and bothersome to you. Reaching beyond your own problems and taking care of others, you gain confidence, courage and a greater sense of calm."

That sounds a lot like love.

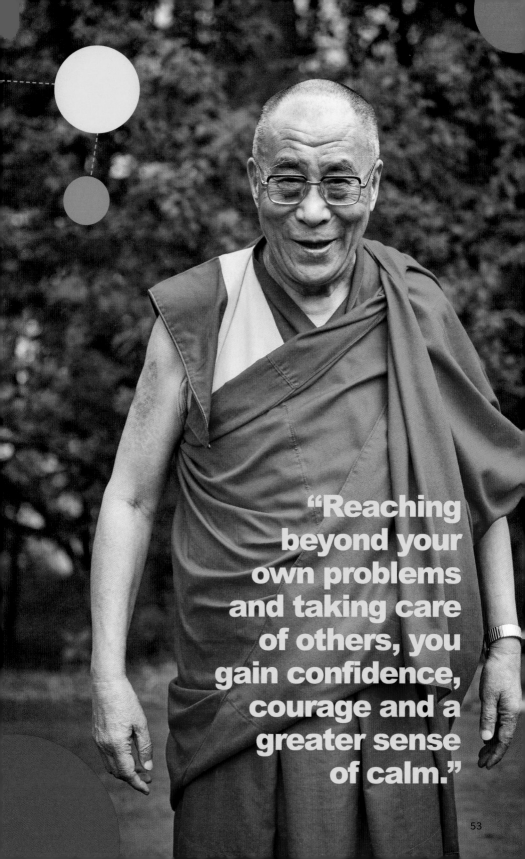

"Reaching beyond your own problems and taking care of others, you gain confidence, courage and a greater sense of calm."

CHAPTER 6

Love's Path

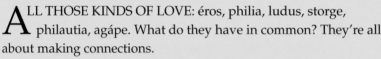

A LL THOSE KINDS OF LOVE: éros, philia, ludus, storge, philautia, agápe. What do they have in common? They're all about making connections.

As people, we spend much of our lives trying to connect with others. Feeling connected makes us feel whole. We are meant to be social, to work together, and to love and care for one another.

Philautia, self-love, might sound boring, but it gives you the foundation you need to love others. *Éros,* romantic love, might be what pop culture obsesses over because it's so intense (it makes for some good stories and songs). It might be messy, and it can get us into trouble. But it also pushes us to care deeply about someone else, to think beyond ourselves. *Agápe,* selfless love, might seem unrealistic sometimes. But if we start small, we can learn to be more loving (and probably happier).

Ripples of Love

All these types of love are parts of the same thing, like ripples in a lake that start at the center—with you—and expand out. First, love yourself. Take care of yourself. Know who you are, and treat that person with kindness and respect. From there, you will have the strength and confidence for healthy relationships. A healthy you can better care for your friends and family. To extend your love further into altruism, practice empathy. Practice forgiveness. Find ways to use your own special talents to help others. Like those ripples in a lake bouncing off the shoreline, love extended outward has a way of bouncing back to us.

And don't forget the fifth and final stage of love—wholehearted loving. That's the goal of love: to be healthy, whole, and connected to others. Such a goal can seem very far away. But that's OK. The thing is, nobody actually gets to the final place. Nobody is ever "done." That's because, instead of a destination, wholehearted loving is more of a journey down a long and winding road. You might wander off sometimes or take the wrong turn. But you can always choose to find your way back.

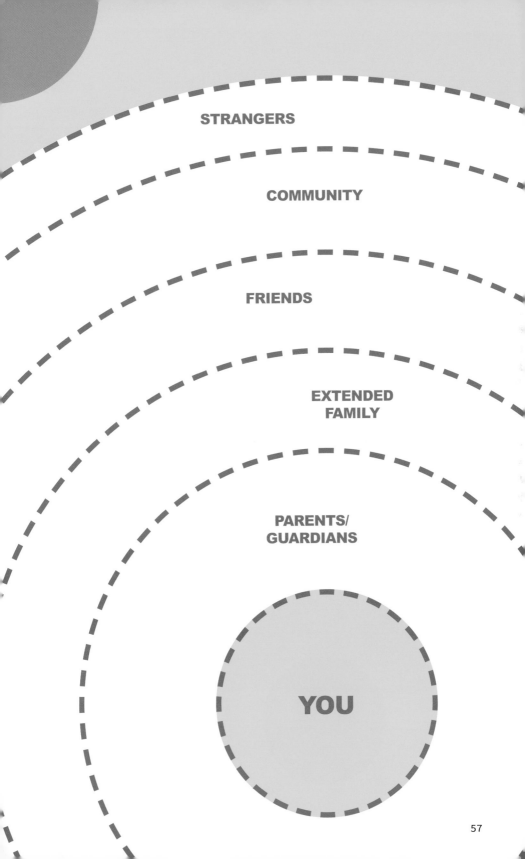

STRANGERS

COMMUNITY

FRIENDS

EXTENDED
FAMILY

PARENTS/
GUARDIANS

YOU

Reach Out

Volunteering is a great way to practice self-love *and* selfless love. It's self-love because it can make you happier and more confident. It's also selfless love because you are helping others. Volunteering gives you a chance to use and improve your skills while making the world a better place.

The best way to volunteer is to give your time to a cause that you care about. Care about the environment? Look for local environmental groups and see how you can help. Passionate about social justice? There's probably a local organization for that too.

If you look around, you can probably find tons of opportunities, big and small. Here are a few examples that might be right for you:

- Collect food for a local food shelf.
- Raise money for an animal shelter by selling baked goods or lemonade.
- Visit a retirement community.
- Pick up litter in your neighborhood.

Work with an adult to find other volunteer programs in your community. These websites let you search for volunteer opportunities for youth based on your interests and skills:

- VolunteerMatch: https://www.volunteermatch.org/
- Youth Volunteer Corps: https://www.yvc.org/

Of course, before you jump into anything, make sure you have a trusted adult on board.

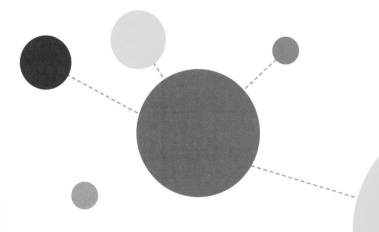

Glossary

affirmation—statement of emotional support or encouragement

altruism—selfless concern for the well-being of others

compassion—concern for the sufferings or misfortunes of others

disillusionment—feeling of disappointment experienced when you realize that something was not as good as you thought it was

dopamine—neurotransmitter that has a strong effect on the brain's reward system. It influences a person's mood and motivation.

empathy—ability to understand and share another's feelings

fMRI—functional magnetic resonance imaging; a medical scan that uses strong magnetic and radio waves to measure brain activity by tracking blood flow

hormone—chemical that travels in the blood and regulates behavior or mood

impulse—strong and sudden desire to do something

mindfulness—awareness of one's mental state

neuron—a nerve cell that transmits information

neurotransmitter—chemical substance between neurons that allows them to communicate

oxytocin—one of the "love hormones," along with vasopressin. Associated with bonding, especially between mother and child.

serotonin—neurotransmitter that helps to regulate sleep, appetite, and mood

values—principles a person holds or what a person thinks is important in life

vasopressin—one of the "love hormones," along with oxytocin. Associated with social bonding.

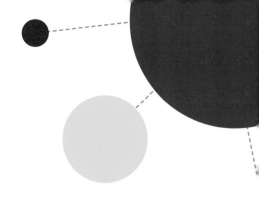

Additional Resources

Further Reading

Chapman, Gary, and Paige Haley Drygas. *A Teen's Guide to the 5 Love Languages: How to Understand Yourself and Improve All Your Relationships.* Chicago: Northfield Publishing, 2016.

Gevinson, Tavin. *Rookie on Love.* New York: Razorbill, 2018.

Watkins, Angela Farris, and Sally Wern Comport. *Love Will See You Through: Martin Luther King Jr.'s Six Guiding Beliefs (as told by his niece).* New York: Simon & Schuster Books for Young Readers, 2014.

Woodson, Jacqueline. *Harbor Me.* New York: Nancy Paulsen Books, 2018.

Zelinger, Laurie E., and Jennifer Kalis. *A Smart Girl's Guide to Liking Herself—Even on the Bad Days: The Secrets to Trusting Yourself, Being Your Best & Never Letting the Bad Days Bring You Down.* Middleton, WI: American Girl, 2012.

Internet Sites

Annie Fox's Blog: Thoughts about Teens, Tweens, Parenting and This Adventure of Living on Earth in the 21st Century
blog.anniefox.com/

New Moon Girls Magazine Body & Feelings Message Board
http://www.nmgmembers.com/messageboards/Body+%26+Feelings

VolunteerMatch
https://www.volunteermatch.org/

Critical Thinking Questions

1

Recall the chemicals discussed in Chapter 2: dopamine, serotonin, testosterone, estrogen, oxytocin, and vasopressin. Pick any two of them. Write about how your behavior toward someone else might change if you had more or less of those two chemicals in your brain.

2

Make a value-affirmation for yourself. Spend some time thinking about what values are most important to you. What are they? Now think of a time when you lived by those values. What happened, and what did you do? Based on your values, write an affirmation that reminds you of who you are.

3

Dr. Martin Luther King Jr. combined his empathy for others with action. He used nonviolent activism to fight against inequality. Think of other examples, large or small, of people who used empathy and action to make the world a better place. Who were they, and what did they do?

Source Notes

p. 6, "the price of love . . ." Barbara J. King. *How Animals Grieve*. Chicago: University of Chicago Press, 2014, p. 8.

p. 13, "way below your cognitive thinking . . ." Helen Fisher, "The Brain in Love," Ted, 2008, https://www.ted.com/talks/helen_fisher_studies _the_brain_in_love?language=en Accessed January 10, 2019.

p. 17, "Romantic love is one of the most . . ." Ibid. Accessed January 10, 2019.

p. 20, "Anthropologists have found evidence . . ." Ibid. Accessed January 10, 2019.

p. 22, "I can't live without . . ." Georgia Arlott, "Inseparable Couple Die Hours Apart on Day of Their 76th Wedding Anniversary," *Mirror*, August 11, 2014, https://www.mirror.co.uk/news/uk -news/inseparable-couple-die-hours-apart-4035320 Accessed January 22, 2019.

p. 22, "disruption of your heart's . . ." "Broken Heart Syndrome," Mayo Clinic, November 5, 2016, https://www.mayoclinic.org/diseases-conditions/ broken-heart-syndrome/diagnosis-treatment/ drc-20354623 Accessed January 22, 2019.

p. 23, "We transformed a meadow vole . . ." Abigail Tucker, "What Can Rodents Tell Us about Why Humans Love?" Smithsonian.com, February 1, 2014, https://www.smithsonianmag.com/ science-nature/what-can-rodents-tell-us-about -why-humans-love-180949441/ Accessed January 22, 2019.

p. 28, "Continue to share your heart . . ." Harvard University, "You Can't Do It Alone," *Harvard Magazine*, March 3, 2014, https://harvardmagazine .com/2011/05/you-cant-do-it-alone Accessed January 10, 2019.

p. 35, "Respect and love go hand in hand . . ." Taura Stinson. *100 Things Every Black Girl Should Know: For Girls 10–100*. Sherman Oaks, CA: Eat Write Hear, 2017, p. 63.

p. 45, "None of you has faith until . . ." Prince Ghazi Bin Muhammad, "The ACW Letter," A Common Word Between Us and You, 2007, https://www .acommonword.com/the-acw-document/ Accessed January 22, 2019.

p. 45, "Love thy neighbor . . ." Vayikra - Leviticus - Chapter 19 (Parshah Kedoshim), Jewish Traditions and Mitzvah Observances, https://www.chabad .org/library/bible_cdo/aid/9920/jewish/ Chapter-19.htm Accessed January 22, 2019.

p. 45, "I tell you, love your enemies . . ." Matthew 5:44, New International Version (NIV), The International Bible Society, https://www.biblica .com/bible/niv/matthew/5/ Accessed January 22, 2019.

p. 45, "radiate boundless love . . ." "Karaniya Metta Sutta: The Discourse on Loving-kindness," The Five Precepts: Pañca-sila, August 29, 2012, https://www .accesstoinsight.org/tipitaka/kn/snp/snp.1.08.piya .html Accessed January 22, 2019.

p. 45, "Love is the steadfast commitment . . ." Cornel West, "Cornel West (@CornelWest)," Twitter, January 3, 2019, https://twitter.com/cornelwest Accessed January 10, 2019.

p. 46, "All those who take up the sword . . ." Matthew 26:52, New American Standard Bible. La Habra, CA: Lockman Foundation, 1995.

p. 47, "When we went on the freedom ride . . ." John Lewis, "Love in Action," interview with Krista Tippet, *On Being*, March 28, 2013, https://onbeing .org/programs/john-lewis-love-in-action-jan2017/ Accessed April 12, 2019.

p. 51, "Compassion training relies on . . ." and "in networks associated to . . ." Olga M. Klimecki, Susanne Leiberg, Matthieu Ricard, and Tania Singer, "Differential Pattern of Functional Brain Plasticity after Compassion and Empathy Training," *Social Cognitive and Affective Neuroscience* 9, no. 6 (2013): 873–79. doi:10.1093/scan/nst060

p. 52, "When you care for others, you manifest . . ." Dalai Lama, "Dalai Lama (@DalaiLama)," Twitter, December 31, 2018. https://twitter.com/ DalaiLama?lang=en Accessed December 31, 2019.

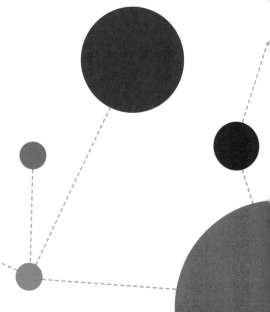

Select Bibliography

Arlott, Georgia, "Inseparable Couple Die Hours Apart on Day of Their 76th Wedding Anniversary," *Mirror*, August 11, 2014, https://www.mirror.co.uk/news/uk-news/inseparable-couple-die-hours-apart-4035320 Accessed January 22, 2019.

Aron, Arthur, Helen Fisher, Debra J. Mashek, Greg Strong, Haifang Li, and Lucy L. Brown, "Reward, Motivation, and Emotion Systems Associated with Early-Stage Intense Romantic Love," *Journal of Neurophysiology* 94, no. 1 (2005): 327–37. doi:10.1152/jn.00838.2004

Bin Muhammad, Prince Ghazi, "The ACW Letter," A Common Word Between Us and You, 2007, https://www.acommonword.com/the-acw-document/ Accessed February 8, 2019.

"Broken Heart Syndrome," Mayo Clinic, November 5, 2016, https://www.mayoclinic.org/diseases-conditions/broken-heart-syndrome/diagnosis-treatment/drc-20354623 Accessed January 22, 2019.

Carroll, Linda. *Love Cycles: The Five Essential Stages of Lasting Love*. Novato, CA: New World Library, 2014.

Ducharme, Jamie, "People Like You More Than You Think, a New Study Suggests," *Time*, September 17, 2018, https://time.com/5396598/good-first-impression/ Accessed January 22, 2019.

Engler, Mark, "When Martin Luther King Jr. Gave up His Guns," *Salon*, January 18, 2014, https://www.salon.com/2014/01/20/when_martin_luther_king_jr_gave_up_his_guns_partner/ Accessed January 22, 2019.

Fisher, Helen, "The Brain in Love," Ted, February 2008, https://www.ted.com/talks/helen_fisher_studies_the_brain_in_love Accessed April 11, 2019.

Fisher, Helen, Arthur Aron, and Lucy L. Brown, "Romantic Love: An fMRI Study of a Neural Mechanism for Mate Choice," *Journal of Comparative Neurology* 493, no. 1 (2005): 58–62. doi:10.1002/cne.20772

Harvard University, "You Can't Do It Alone," *Harvard Magazine*, May 25, 2011, https://harvardmagazine.com/2011/05/you-cant-do-it-alone Accessed March 5, 2019.

hooks, bell. *All About Love: New Visions*. New York: Harper Perennial, 2018.

King, Barbara J. *How Animals Grieve*. Chicago: University of Chicago Press, 2014.

King, Martin Luther, Jr. *Strength to Love*. Philadelphia: Fortress, 1981.

Klimecki, Olga M., Susanne Leiberg, Matthieu Ricard, and Tania Singer, "Differential Pattern of Functional Brain Plasticity after Compassion and Empathy Training," *Social Cognitive and Affective Neuroscience* 9, no. 6 (2013): 873–79. doi:10.1093/scan/nst060

Knapton, Sarah, "Relationships: Opposites Do Not Attract, Scientists Prove," *Telegraph*, February 23, 2016, https://www.telegraph.co.uk/news/science/science-news/12170295/Relationships-opposites-do-not-attract-scientists-prove.html Accessed January 22, 2019.

Krznaric, Roman, "The Ancient Greeks' 6 Words for Love (And Why Knowing Them Can Change Your Life)," *YES!*, August 14, 2018, https://www.yesmagazine.org/happiness/the-ancient-greeks-6-words-for-love-and-why-knowing-them-can-change-your-life Accessed January 22, 2019.

Lewis, John, "Love in Action," interview with Krista Tippet, *On Being*, March 28, 2013, https://onbeing.org/programs/john-lewis-love-in-action-jan2017/ Accessed April 12, 2019.

Miller, John P. *Love and Compassion: Exploring Their Role in Education*. Toronto, ON: University of Toronto Press, 2018.

Ricard, Matthieu, Charlotte Mandell, and Sam Gordon. *Altruism: The Power of Compassion to Change Yourself and the World*. New York: Back Bay Books, 2015.

Schüz, Natalie, and Benjamin Schüz, "Self-Affirmation: Protecting the Self and Protecting Subjective Well-Being," *The Happy Mind: Cognitive Contributions to Well-Being*, 2017, 291–308. doi:10.1007/978-3-319-58763-9_16

Stinson, Taura. *100 Things Every Black Girl Should Know: For Girls 10–100*. Sherman Oaks, CA: Eat, Write, Hear, 2017.

Tucker, Abigail, "What Can Rodents Tell Us About Why Humans Love?" Smithsonian.com, February 1, 2014, https://www.smithsonianmag.com/science-nature/what-can-rodents-tell-us-about-why-humans-love-180949441/ Accessed January 22, 2019.

Yue, Carole, "Reward Pathway in the Brain," Khan Academy, https://www.khanacademy.org/science/health-and-medicine/mental-health/drug-abuse-and-drug-addictions/v/reward-pathway-in-the-brain Accessed January 10, 2019.

Zelinger, Laurie E., and Jennifer Kalis. *A Smart Girl's Guide to Liking Herself—Even on the Bad Days: The Secrets to Trusting Yourself, Being Your Best & Never Letting the Bad Days Bring You Down*. Middleton, WI: American Girl, 2012.

Index

About the Author

Matt Lilley lives and writes in Minneapolis, Minnesota. He has written five books for young people. His favorite topics to write about include health issues, nature, and exploration. He loves learning about topics in science and sharing that knowledge. Matt has a master's degree in scientific and technical communication. He is also a Minnesota Master Naturalist. He loves going out in nature and seeing what's out there. To find out more about Matt, visit him at mattlilley.ink.